THE WRITING OF
ECONOMICS

Books by Donald N. McCloskey

Economic Maturity and Entrepreneurial Decline:
British Iron and Steel, 1870–1913

Enterprise and Trade in Victorian Britain:
Essays in Historical Economics

The Applied Theory of Price (Macmillan)

The Rhetoric of Economics

Econometric History

THE WRITING OF
ECONOMICS

Donald N. McCloskey

DEPARTMENTS OF ECONOMICS AND OF HISTORY
UNIVERSITY OF IOWA

MACMILLAN PUBLISHING COMPANY
NEW YORK
COLLIER MACMILLAN PUBLISHERS
LONDON

Macmillan Publishing Company
866 Third Avenue, New York, New York 10022

Collier Macmillan Canada, Inc.

LIBRARY OF CONGRESS CATALOGING-IN-PUBLICATION DATA

McCloskey, Donald N.
    The writing of economics.

    Bibliography: p.
    Includes index.
    1. English language—Rhetoric.   2. Economics—
Authorship.   I. Title.
PE1479.E35M33   1987   808'.06633   86-12678
ISBN 0-02-379520-4

Printing: 1 2 3 4 5 6 7   Year: 7 8 9 0 1 2 3

ISBN   0-02-379520-4

Acknowledgments

The implied reader of this book is a student of economics or of related fields in business or the social sciences who needs to write.

I thank a group of real readers, and good writers, who have improved it by telling me where it was wrong or right: Eleanor Birch, Thomas Borcherding, Wilma R. Ebbitt, Ross Echert, Clifford Geertz, Douglas F. Greer, Albert Hirschman, Sara Hirschman, Jack Hirshleifer, Linda Kerber, Charles Kindleberger, Meir Kohn, David Landes, much of the McCloskey family (Laura, Helen, and Joanne), Joel Mokyr, Erin Newton, much of the Solow family (John, Barbara, and Robert), Richard Sutch, Donald Sutherland, John R. Trimble, Steven Webb, A. Wick, and Barbara Yerkes. It is a good piece of advice, which students seldom have time to follow, to get someone to criticize a piece of writing early. Better to be criticized harshly in private, and fix what is wrong, than to be massacred in public.

The book originated a long time ago in a course for students at the University of Chicago. I thank the students for their help. An earlier version directed at young teachers of economics appeared under the same title in the April 1985 issue of *Economic Inquiry*. I thank the editor for permission to use parts of it.

In bringing the book to print Anthony English at Macmillan was his tasteful and energetic self. Cathy Hansen gave it a good student's-eye reading. Marguerite Knoedel, who typed the many drafts, knows that I'm not kidding when I say that even passable writing involves rewriting again and again and again. I read the other day that Hemingway rewrote the last page of *Farewell to Arms* sixty times. Sixty. The John Simon Guggenheim Foundation, the National Endowment for the Humanities, the Institute for Advanced Study, and the University of Iowa gave me the time to rewrite the book into its present form.

D. N. M.

Contents

THE WRITING OF
ECONOMICS

Why You Should Not Stop Reading Here

The man in the street favors his mistaken opinions about free trade, and will not listen to professional argument. His opinions are his very own after all: free trade is "just a matter of opinion." Anyone is "entitled to his opinion in a free country." Fooey to the professionals.

The man in the street is a lot like the writer of economics, or other writers of technical matter. Although they write a lot, most writers of economics have the man-in-the-street's attitude toward what they write. They seldom rewrite. They don't look into professional advice on writing. They admire what they write, favoring their mistakes as God-given and personal, just matters of opinion.

Now it's true that you can't change your body type or basic character, and it's therefore offensive for some louse to criticize them:

Linus: What's this?

Lucy: This is something to help you be a better person next year. . . . This is a list I made up of *all* your faults. [EXIT]

Linus [reading, increasingly indignant]: Faults? You call these *faults*? These aren't faults! These are *character traits*!

The amateurs suppose that writing is like body type or character. But the professionals in writing, such as poets and newspaper writers, have learned to take advantage of criticism. The amateurs by contrast don't view criticism as something to take advantage of. They react badly to it. If someone says that it's clumsy to use "not only . . . but also" or phony to use "prioritize" they are liable to react the way they react to remarks about their body shape. Heh, that's who I am; lay off, you creep.

The first and final truth about writing is that we all—you, I, and J. K. Galbraith—can use more criticism. We would be a lot more professional if we did.

1. *Writing Is the Economist's Trade*

In a "Shoe" strip the uncle bird comes in the front door with a briefcase overflowing with paper and says to the nephew bird, "I'm exhausted, but I've got to work: I've got to get this report out by tomorrow morning." Next panel: "I'll be up until 3:00 writing it." Last panel, the nephew pictured with a horrified look on his face: "You mean homework is *forever*?!"

Yes, son, homework is forever, and much of it is writing. No one tells the beginner in this trade with a lot of writing how important it is to write well. Noneconomists have been complaining about economic and other social scientific writing for decades (Williamson, 1947), but there is supposed to be no economic reward for listening to noneconomists. Older economists mainly shrug off their responsibility to teach the young how to write, offering the strange excuse that the young won't pay attention. (You'll recall that no such lack of attention could stop them from explaining the income and substitution effects in three different ways.) Sometimes a government agency or another employer of economists will for a while fall into the hands of someone who cares about writing. But then it falls back into other hands, and the "report" consisting mainly of summaries and outlines of itself comes back into favor. Only a few economists have written about economic writing. Walter Salant did his part in an essay published in 1969. And J. K. Galbraith wrote in 1978 on "Writing, Typing and Economics." (He was taking off on Hemingway's crack about a bad writer: "That's not writing: that's typing." A lot of economics isn't very good typing.) Thin pickings.

The lack of interest in writing does not come from a lack of importance. A big secret in economics is that good writing pays well and bad writing pays badly. Honest. Rotten writing causes more papers and reports to fail than do rotten statistics or rotten research. You have to be read to be listened to. Bad writing is not read, even by the professors or bosses paid to read it. Can you imagine actually *reading* the worst paper you've ever turned in? Your sainted mother herself wouldn't be able to stand it.

Economics teachers teach things slightly off the point. The courses don't tell you directly how to do economics—they tell you about it, but not how to do it—and most programs offer little in the way of on-the-job practice. This is so throughout the program. Students are taught minor details in statistics, when the hard business of quantitative thinking in economics is getting the data straight; they are taught minor details in mathematics, when the hard business of mathematical economics is getting economic ideas straight. In most schools they are taught nothing about writing, when the hard business of economic thinking is getting the words straight. The master craftsman turns his back on the apprentice, concealing each skill of the trade, such as how to cut a board clean.

The reason for learning to cut it clean, I repeat, is that the skill is used a lot. What economists do (and what people educated in economics do) depends on writing, because writing is the cheapest way to reach a big audience and because writing forces the writer to think. An economically trained person is likely to spend most of his or her working life writing papers, reports, memoranda, proposals, columns, and letters. Economics depends much more on writing (and on speaking, another neglected art) than on the mathematics and statistics usually touted as the tools of the trade. Most of the economist's skills are verbal. An economist should be embarrassed to do such a large part of the craft unprofessionally. Shame on us.

2. *Writing Is Thinking*

The answer will come: "Oh, that's just a matter of style: after all, it's content that matters." Students will sometimes complain about bad grades earned for writing badly, arguing that they had the *content* right, or that they *meant* to say the right thing (people who are complaining speak in italics).

Anybody who wants to be heard, though, will want to express her content well. Bad writing, to say it again, does not get read. The only bad prose that you literally must read comes from the Internal Revenue Service. All other writers are on sufferance, competing minute-by-minute with other writers or with the television show or with the chance to get to bed a little early tonight. The writer who wants to keep her audience will keep in mind that the audience can at any moment get up and leave.

The influence of style is greater than you might think. The history of ideas has many wide turns caused by "mere" lucidity and elegance of expression. Three and a half centuries ago Galileo's *Dialogo* persuaded people that the earth went around the sun, but not because it was a Copernican tract (there were others) or because it contained much new evidence (it did not). It was persuasive because it was a masterpiece of Italian prose. Poincaré's good French and Einstein's good German early in this century were no small contributors to their influence on mathematics and physics. To turn back to economics, John Maynard Keynes hypnotized three generations of economists and politicians with his graceful fluency in English.*

The premise that you can split content from expression is wrong. They are yoke and white in a scrambled egg. Economically speaking the production function for thinking cannot be written as the sum of two subfunctions, one "producing results" and the other "writing them up." The function is not separable.

You do not learn the details of an argument until writing it in detail, and in writing the details you uncover flaws in the fundamentals. Thinking *is* detail: you can't add 2,654 and 2,765 if you get all fuzzy about whether 2 plus 2 equals 4 or 5. You have to know it for sure. Good thinking is accurate, symmetrical, relevant to the thoughts of the audience, concrete yet usefully abstract, concise yet usefully full; above all it

---

* Keynes is universally acknowledged as the best writer that economics has had. See, however, the hostile dissection of the style of a passage from Keynes in Graves and Hodge [1943 (1961), pp. 332–340]. It makes one wince, that the best is so easy to fault.

is self-critical and honest. So too is good writing. Good writers in economics write self-critically and honestly, trying to say what they mean. They often find out that what looked persuasive when floating vaguely in the mind looks foolish when moored to the page. Better, they find truths they didn't know they had. They sharpen their fuzzy notion of an obstacle to trade by finding the right word to describe it; they see the other side of a market by writing about the demand side with clarity. Writing resembles mathematics. Mathematics is a language, an instrument of communication. But so also is language a mathematics, an instrument of thought.

3. *Rules Can Help, But Bad Rules Hurt*

Like mathematics, writing can be learned. It's an evasion to talk of writing as a natural gift, a free lunch from the gods. The notion seems to be that if you grovel before the genius of Mark Twain or George Orwell you don't have to look at your own writing critically. "Gosh, they were such swell writers! Me, well, I'm just a jerk." The natural-gift theory does not let you out. Although few can become Mark Twains or George Orwells anyone can write better. Twain and Orwell, in fact, devoted considerable effort to explaining how (Twain, 1895; Orwell, 1946).

Elementary writing can be learned like high school algebra. On the simplest level neither is inborn. Only a few people can prove important new theorems in mathematics, about as few as can write regularly for the *New Yorker*. Yet anyone can learn to solve a set of simultaneous equations, just as anyone can learn to delete a quarter of the words from the first draft. Like mathematics at the simplest level, good writing at the simplest level follows rules. *

---

* There are scores of manuals on English writing, most of them pretty good. My three favorites, from elementary to advanced, are William Strunk, Jr. and E. B. White, *The Elements of Style* (1959 and later editions); Robert Graves and Alan Hodge, *The Reader Over Your Shoulder: A Handbook for Writers of English Prose* (1943 and later editions); and Joseph M. Williams, *Style: Ten Lessons in Clarity and Grace* (1981). Three college texts I know

Don't believe everyone who sets up as a teacher of the rules. The first correct rule is that many of the rules we learned in Miss Jones' class in the eighth grade are wrong. Sometimes of course Miss Jones had a point. For example, dangling out on a limb alone, she justly castigated participles badly placed in a sentence. Yet in other ways her list of rules and the folk wisdom that reinforced it have hurt.

"Never repeat the same word or phrase within three lines," said Miss Jones, and because the rule fitted splendidly with our budding verbosity at age 13 we adopted it as the habit of a lifetime. Now we can't mention the "consumer" in one line without an itch to call it the "household" in the next and the "decisionmaker" in the next. Our readers slip down into a fog known in the writing trade as "elegant variation." "Never write 'I'," wrote she, and we (and you and I) have drowned in "we" ever since, a "we" less suited to mere economists than to kings, editors, and people with tapeworms. "Don't be common; emulate James Fenimore Cooper; writing well is writing swell," said she—more by the way she praised Harry Whimple and his fancy talk than by outright rule—and in later life we struggled to attain a splendidly dignified bureaucratese.

Miss Jones ruled against our urge to freely split infinitives. H. W. Fowler, who wrote in 1926 an amusing book on the umpromising subject of *Modern English Usage*, knew how to handle her [1926 (1965) article "Split Infinitives"]: "Those who neither know nor care [what a split infinitive is] are the vast majority, and are a happy folk, to be envied by most. . . . 'to really understand' comes readier to their lips and pens than 'really to understand'; they see no reason why they should not

and admire are Donald Hall, *Writing Well* (1979); Richard A. Lanham; *Revising Prose* (1987); and Sheridan Baker and David Hamilton, *The Complete Stylist* (1987). Some more advanced books are F. L. Lucas, *Style* (1955); Jacques Barzun, *Simple and Direct: A Rhetoric for Writers* (1976); Part III of Jacques Barzun and Henry F. Graff, *The Modern Researcher* (1970); Paul R. Halmos, pp. 19–48 in Norman E. Steenrod, *et al.*, *How to Write Mathematics* (1973); Sir Ernest Gowers, *The Complete Plain Words* (1962 and subsequent editions); Howard S. Becker, *Writing for Social Scientists* (1986).

say it (small blame to them, seeing that reasons are not their critics' strong point)."

Miss Jones filled us with guilt about using a preposition to end a sentence with. Winston Churchill, a politician of note who wrote English well, knew how to handle her, and the editor who meddled with his preposition-ended sentence: "This is the sort of impertinence up with which I will not put."

Worst of all Miss Jones fastened onto our impressionable minds the terrible, iterative rule of Jonesian arrangement: "Say what you're going to say; say it; say that you've said it." The Jones rule has nearly ruined economic prose. Most unpublished papers in economics consist of summary, outline, anticipation, announcement, repetition, and review. They never get to the point.

4. *Be Thou Clear*

The one genuine rule, a golden one, is Be Clear. In the first century after Christ a Roman professor of writing and speaking put it this way (Quintilian, Book VIII, ii, 24): "Therefore one ought to take care to write not merely so that the reader can understand but so that he cannot possibly misunderstand." Clarity is a social matter, not something to be decided unilaterally by the writer. The reader like the consumer is sovereign. If the reader thinks something you write is unclear then it is, by definition. Quit arguing. Karl Popper, a philosopher with a good style and a correspondingly wide influence, wrote:

> I. . . learned never to defend anything I had written against the accusation that it is not clear enough. If a conscientious reader finds a passage unclear, it has to be rewritten. . . . I write, as it were, with somebody constantly looking over my shoulder and constantly pointing out to me passages that are not clear. (1976, p. 83).

Clarity is a matter of speed directed at the point. Bad writing stops you with a puzzle in every other sentence. It sends you off in irrelevant directions. It distracts you from the point, provoking irritated questions about what the subject is now, what the connection might be with the subject a moment ago, and why the words differ. You are always losing your way. Bad writing makes slow reading. The practice of Graves and Hodge [1943 (1961)] in compiling the bad examples for their principles of Clear and Graceful Expression was "to glance at every book or paper we found lying about and, whenever our reading pace was checked by some difficulty of expression, to note the cause" (p. 127). (The sentence itself, incidentally, illustrates one rule of reading pace they could have followed better: Do Not Overpunctuate.)

In most writing the reader is in trouble more than half the time. You can see this by watching your own troubles. Notice in the present long and involved sentence, since there is a lot of clumsy intrusion of new stuff and the jumps in elevation of lingo, how no one could follow it, at least on first reading without having to go over it once or twice, because anyway it is ungrammatical, which means not only that it breaks a Miss Jones rule but also that it confuses you and anyone else who happens to be reading by violating your expectations, and that it has too much in it anyway, with no nice arrangement, which would make sense of it. You stumble and yawn and wander when you read such stuff.

Reading your own writing cold, a week after drafting it, will show you places where even you cannot follow the sense. Knock such places into shape. If the reader has too much trouble he gives up. Lack of clarity is selfish and confusing. The writer is wasting the reader's time. Up with this the reader need not put.

Telling someone who hasn't thought much about it to "Be Clear," though, is no help. It has been said that "It is as hard to write well as to be good." In the abstract the golden rule of writing clearly helps about as much as the other golden rule, of which it is a corollary. "All things whatsoever ye would that men should do to you, do ye even so to them." Well, sure, yes, all right; but how?

5. *The Rules Are Factual Rather Than Logical*

The rules come from observation. In the best writing you do not hit many sentences where the reading stops or where your ear is damaged by noise. It's no trick to spot the bad sentences and to see what went wrong. Just read. You feel it, like sunshine or rain. You the reader know that George Orwell wrote well, that you seldom have difficulty understanding what Tom Wolfe is talking about, that Mary McCarthy doesn't take many false steps. As Johnson said two centuries ago of Addison: He who would acquire a good style should devote his days and night to the study of Orwell, Wolfe, and McCarthy.

In recent economics, on a rather lower level, the list would include Akerlof, Arrow, Boulding, Bronfenbrenner, Buchanan, Caves, Clower, L. Davis, Fogel, Friedman, Haberler, Harberger, Heilbroner, Hirschman, Hughes, Galbraith, Gerschenkron, Griliches, Harry Johnson, Keynes, Kindleberger, Lebergott, Leijonhufvud, Olson, Parker, Robertson, J. Robinson, Rostow, Schelling, Schumpeter, Schultz, Solow, Stigler, Tobin, Tullock, and Yeager. When you read any of these in economics, pay attention: this is as good as it gets. Yet the diminishing returns are painfully sharp. Even economists who take care with their style will overuse "we," the passive voice, and fancytalk from Latin and Greek ("We perceive that equilibrium is achieved by a process of successive approximations").

You can't define good style without a list. Good style is what good writers do. Double negatives, for example, aren't "illogical" (modern French and ancient Greek have them); they are social mistakes, at least right now. If Orwell and his kind started using "I ain't no fool," no amount of schoolmaster logic should stand in the way of its imitation. In matters of taste the main standard is the practice of good people. Furthermore, everything from the standard of proof in number theory to the standard of skill in baton twirling is a matter of taste. You tell who is good by comparing good with bad.

Reading becomes more efficient if it grades writers by stylistic competence. The violation of the rules of clarity and grace send a signal of incompetence. If double negatives begin to be used by writers who write well in other ways—who say persuasive things, for instance, and say them plainly—then the double negative will lose its value as a signal of incompetence. Because the violations signal incompetence they are correlated with each other: it's a good bet that a writer who does not know how to express parallel ideas in parallel form, and does not care, will also not know how to avoid excessive summarization and anticipation; it is about as good a bet that he will not know how to think, and will not care.

These features of good and bad style are perfectly "objective," which is to say that lists of rules are not "just one man's opinion." "Objectively" (the word is philosophically silly, incidentally) we can measure the characteristics of writing that determine its readability. The rules of taste that we can't measure are as definite as the rules of baseball. Competent players of the language game know many of them by rote, and can sense when one they do not know by rote is being violated. The competent writers, of course, write with competent readers in mind. The test of rules is excellent practice, and the test of practice is the sovereign reader.

6. *Classical Rhetoric Guides Even the Economical Writer*

Essays are made from bunches of paragraphs, which are made from bunches of sentences, which are made from bunches of words. Before you start an essay choose a subject that meets the assignment yet stirs something in your soul (you cannot work on a subject unless you love it or hate it; you should therefore do your economic history on baseball and your industrial organization on advertising). The rules about whole essays or paragraphs are most useful at the stage of first composition; the rules about sentences and words at the stage of final revision. Some rules apply everywhere: it is good to be brief in the whole essay and in the single word, during the midnight fever of composition and during the morning chill of revision. Brevity is the soul of clarity, too. Yet the rules of writing can be stuffed if necessary into boxes by diminishing size from essay to word.

What is needed for this is an economic rhetoric. I do not mean by "rhetoric" a frill, or a device for lying—the politician's "heated rhetoric" at a news conference or the professor's "bad rhetoric" when arguing a weak case. I mean the whole art of argument, which is its classical and correct meaning. It is the art, as Wayne Booth put it (1974, p. 59), "of discovering warrantable beliefs and improving those beliefs in shared discourse."

The three important parts of classical rhetoric were Invention, Arrangement, and Style. Invention, the framing of arguments worth listening to, is the business of economic theory and of empirical economics. Theory and empirical economics seem to be doing all right, although they have been hurt by an official methodology, which rhetoric can counteract (McCloskey, 1986).

Rhetoric helps to see, for instance, that an economic argument is a series of analogies. Saying that the market for automobiles is "just like" a diagram of demand and supply is, when you think about it, bizarre. Not false: bizarre. It is also bizarre to compare a woman to a summer's day, but Shakespeare did it, exploring its persuasiveness. Economic models are economic poetry.

The economic poems make remarks about each other, as poems do. Once you have solved one problem by stating it as an analogy you can use the problem as an analogy for others, a great aid to Invention. Suppose you come to understand that a waitress who customarily gets tips is not necessarily better off because of the custom: without tipping she would have to get a higher salary to retain her and others in the industry. The analogy here is of waitresses to business tycoons or gold dealers. Once you have grasped the primary analogy you can see others later as analogies in turn to it. Someone says, "Miners are made better off by safety regulations." You think: "Ah, hah! That's just the Tipped Waitress Problem," and then say out loud, astonishing your audience with your economic inventiveness, "No, without the safety regulations they would be paid more: so only the miners who value health highly compared to money are benefited." You have used analogy, part of the rhetoric of economics. It's the main way that economists approach this first part of classical rhetoric, Invention, the getting of ideas.

Arrangement, too, the arranging of ideas, is a part of economic rhetoric not much examined. A good deal of economic prose implies that the only proper arrangement of an empirical essay is Introduction, Outline of the Rest of the Paper, The Theory, The (Linear) Model, The Results, Suggestions for Future Research (since nothing ever works), and (again) Summary. One rarely sees experiments with alternative arrangements, such as dialogues or reports on the actual sequence of the author's discovery. At any rate one does not see them in print. When economists talk among themselves, in the seminar room or hallway, the dialogue is the whole point, usually introduced by a report in sequence of "how I actually came to this subject." Economists might try learning good Arrangement from their own behavior.

An official arrangement has spread to the social sciences from physics and biology. It is supposed to make social sciences more scientific to have a section entitled "Data" or "Results." This official rhetoric is a poor one. It does not tell what needs to be known—which experiments failed, what mathematics proved fruitless, why exactly the questions were asked in the way they were (see Medawar, 1964). It is much better to make your own outline, one that fits your argument.

7. *Fluency Can Be Achieved by Grit*

The third branch of classical rhetoric, Style, is easier to teach, and is therefore the rest of the subject here.

Style begins with mere fluency, getting the stuff down on paper. And it ends with revising, again and again, until you've taken out every snare and ugliness. You will have done some research (this is known as "thinking") and are sitting down to write. Sitting down to write can be a problem, for it is then that your subconscious, which is dismayed by the anxiety of filling up blank pieces of paper, suggests that it would be ever so much more fun to do the dishes or to go down to get the mail. Sneak up on it and surprise it with the ancient recipe for success in intellectual pursuits: locate chair; apply rear end to it; locate writing implement; use it.* Once planted at the desk, though, you will find your subconscious drawing on various

---

* You may wish to increase the element of surprise by writing standing at a tall desk, as my colleague Gary Fethke does.

reserves of strength to persuade you to stop: fear, boredom, the impulse to track down that trivial point by adjourning to the library. Time to go see Mary or John. Time to watch the basketball game. Time to get some fresh air. Don't. Resist. It's time to write.

A strange one of these distractions is taste. The trouble with developing good taste in writing (which is the point of studying books like this one) is that you begin to find your stuff distasteful. This creates doubt. Waves of doubt—the conviction that everything you've done so far is rubbish—will wash over you from time to time. The only help is a cheerful faith that more work will raise even this rubbish up to your newly acquired standards. Once achieved, you can reraise the standards and acquire better doubt at a level of still better taste. Buck up. Irrational cheerfulness is hard to teach but good to learn for any serious work.

8. *Write Too Early Rather Than Too Late*

The teachable trick is getting a first draft. Don't wait until the research is done to begin writing because writing, to repeat, is a way of thinking. Be writing all the time, working on a page or two here, a section there. Research *is* writing.

(I'd better write here parenthetically a word or two about the fraternity file or the "research services" that will write your paper for you. The word is "Don't." Or maybe "Immoral." Or perhaps "Idiotic." Certainly "Ripoff," for everyone involved except the services themselves. A student who tries to steal or buy his degree will cheapen the degree his classmates earn, the way professors who give all As cheapen it or the students who cheat on exams cheapen it. Maybe that's the best word: "Cheap.")

As a real student you will have notes, bits of prose to be placed in the mosaic. It helps to give each note a title stating its point. Though any writing surface from clay tablet to CRT screen can hold the notes, white 4 × 6-inch cards lined on one side are best. Vladimir Nabokov wrote even novels with cards. Cards fit expository prose well. The smaller 3 × 5-inch cards are too small to hold a rounded idea, even if allowed to spill onto the back; the bigger 5 × 8-inch cards are too big to carry around while awaiting the moment of inspiration in the library or classroom or street. Use one idea per card, even if the idea is only a single line. It's a mistake to economize by cramming several ideas on one card, because then you can't rearrange them. Forget about the wasted paper. You only save a few cents.

Manila folders are nice, as are the fancier folders with Garfield and other figures of mythology on them. They can hold longer ideas, fuller outlines, bulkier computer output, and bigger bunches of cards. The sociologist C. Wright Mills wrote an exhilarating essay in 1959, "On Intellectual Crafts-manship," in which he called the whole set of cards, folders, and so forth The File (p. 196): "You must set up a file, which is, I suppose, a sociologist's way of saying: Keep a journal. Many creative writers keep journals; the sociologist's [and economist's] need for systematic reflection demands it." It should become thick and rich, dumped out occasionally and rearranged.

Read through the file (which is Invention) trying to see an outline in it (which is Arrangement). The first outline will be broad. Allocate the cards to related stacks; add cards reminding you of transitions and new ideas that occur as you ponder the file. If the broad outline does not come easily, write down a few words per card on a sheet of paper and try to see a pattern. Arrangement is like good statistical work, searching the data for patterns. It's like good dramatic work, too, searching the audience for response. Your arrangement should be artful.

Now set aside the broad outline, keeping it steadily in mind. You need it as a goal to give the writing direction. You can change it, and should do so as the essay takes shape. Pick a little part of the outline to write about today. It need not be the beginning, although it's sometimes difficult to write first drafts any other way. The paper should be a story because readers normally read from beginning to end. List on another sheet in a word or two the detailed, paragraph-level points suggested by the cards or by the file or, best of all, by the mad, creative file in your brain. You need a certain intensity for all this. Make yourself care. Writing cannot be done as a routine, like peeling potatoes.

Write still another outline, an even narrower one about the points you are going to write in the next few sentences, checking off the points as you write (Arrangement is a matter of finding good outlines, from the level of the book down to the level of the paragraph). The points in all outlines from broad to narrow should be substantive, not formal: not "Introduction" or "Concluding Paragraph" but "Economists pay no attention to the sexual division of labor" and "Housework should be included in national income"; or in a telegraphic style, "div. lab." and "housewk & GNP." Keep another piece of paper at hand to try out turns of phrase or to note down ideas that occur in advance of their use. When you get an inspiration do not depend on your memory to keep it. A phrase or word will jog it. Don't let the moment pass.

9. *You Will Need Tools*

You will therefore need several pieces of paper scattered around all the time, with the outline sitting there, too, covered with notes for revision, and your File standing in readiness at a distance. Don't worry about being neat: clean up in a dull moment. To repeat, do not save paper. Leave plenty of room on the page for revision. Writing on both sides is bad economy because it makes it impossible to cut up drafts or to add things on the simplest place, which is the back. View paper as working capital, not something that you want to use sparingly.

You will need certain other bits of capital in abundance. Pencils are in general better than pens, although it's pleasant to shift from time to time. You should find pleasure in exercising the tools of writing. An expensive and well balanced fountain pen is old-fashioned, to be sure, but amusing to use when the mood strikes. Indulge yourself. Some day in this spirit I'm going to buy a Mont Blanc pen ($200 a copy), then try not to lose it. On the other hand, don't become compulsive about equipment and procedures and surroundings. Ernest Hemingway used to sharpen forty pencils with a jackknife before beginning to write. He didn't publish enough. Be more flexible than this if you can manage it. Look on yourself as an honest-to-goodness professional writer (which is what you are) who can do any job on command anywhere with any equipment whatsoever, Ernie Pyle pecking out dispatches on a portable Olivetti from a fox hole on the Italian front.

Many people compose at a typewriter or in these latter days a computer screen. Some dictate into a tape recorder. A new medium will change your style, perhaps for the better. Switching from medium to medium is worth trying, because each medium suggests new ways of putting the matter. Pencil is forgiving, ink on paper less so, type still less, and recording tape least of all.

The word processor is at a different level entirely, a new and higher production function. Any writer who does not use a word processor is wasting a lot of time, although perhaps sparing the world some ill-considered fluency. Even bad typists find composing on word processors almost excessively easy. The machines do not resist as much as typewriters and are entirely forgiving of mistakes.

When using an unforgiving medium your style will be arranged point by point in a straight line. This can be a good thing for your style if it tends otherwise to overdecoration with insertion and adjective, although it will tend also to be erroneous in detail and harder to rewrite. When writing by hand or typewriter always double- or triple-space: style in writing, as was said earlier and will be said again, is rewriting. You need room for it. The word processor, of course, solves this problem, too.

The next most important tool is a dictionary. Every place you read or write should have its own dictionary. Do not use the crummy little paperback dictionaries: they do not lie flat and therefore require two hands to use. Use the big college dictionaries, which you can get cheap at second-hand stores and scatter around your place (being up-to-date is unimportant in a dictionary). A good one is *Webster's* [nearly all American dictionaries are "Webster's," which reduces the value of the signal to zero] *New World Dictionary of the American Language*, Second College Edition (1976 and other dates). It is handsomely produced, does a good job at word origins, notes Americanisms (handy when writing to non-Americans), gives easy-to-follow pronunciation guides (handy when speaking to Americans), and distinguishes levels of usage. The big Merriam-Webster *Third Webster's International* is not good, because it does not tell you what usage good writers prefer. Its college offsprings (*Webster's New Collegiate Dictionary* and siblings) are therefore suspect. *

A dictionary is more than a spelling list. Pause to read the definitions and the word origins. Part of the purpose again is to write well in the elementary sense of avoiding embarrassing mistakes in usage. If you think "disinterested" means the same thing as "uninterested," for instance, you need to get acquainted with a dictionary urgently, and start reading good writing with it at hand. Yet beyond what is meet and proper (look up "meet," noting that in this sense it is related to "medical"), wordlore will make you grow. Malcolm X educated himself in prison by memorizing a dictionary. Learn to like words and to inquire into their backgrounds. It is a useful friendship and a joy of life.

English spelling could drive anyone nuts. George Bernard Shaw noted once that you could spell the word "fish" in English as "ghoti" ("gh" as in enou*gh*, "o" as in w*o*men, and "ti" as in na*ti*on). It is astonishing that anyone learns to spell according to Webster. In the sixteenth century nobody much cared, and Shakespeare (Shakspere, Shakespere) spelt 'em as hee plees'd. By now, however, you must spell according to Webster or you will look like a jerk. It's stupid and unfair but

---

* My colleague Eleanor Birch recalls a reviewer's verse on The Third: "That I imply and you infer / Is clear to me; but don't refer / To Webster's Third, which may imply / It's all the same to you and I." The big old Second (1934 and later editions) is a wonderful book, filled with scholarship and loony trivia. Any word person ought to try to own it. Incidentally, it's easy to own the great *Oxford English Dictionary*, published originally in twelve large volumes: join the Book-of-the-Month Club (fulfill your contract, but I can't recommend the books) and get the microprint edition in two bigger volumes and a reading glass for twenty-five bucks. The "OED," as those in the know call it, tells how every English word has been used since the beginning: the word "word," for example, takes up thirteen big columns.

that's the way things are. Students chronically misspell a few words, such as "receive" (remember: i before e except after c; but what about "leisure," "either," or "weird"?), "separate" (pronounce carefully the adjective form of the word—a separate peace—and you'll remember it), schedule (which I could not spell until graduate school), whether (as against rain and shine), their (as against over there or where they're).

A good book for those demoralized by their inability to spell according to Webster is Norman Lewis, A *Dictionary of Correct Spelling*, which patiently explains under the wrong spelling why some words are -able and some -ible. Don't fret: everyone else misspells, too. Just work on it. For years I have had to look up "misspells" every time I wanted to use it on a student paper (you can see why I had to get it right); I'm working now on learning "questionnaire" (two n's) and "imitation" (one m). Make a list of your own and start getting the words into your mind's eye.

A thesaurus (Greek: "treasure") finds the precise word within a more or less fuzzy region of the language. Use a big one, not the pocket versions. The best is *Roget's International Thesaurus*. If you are unskilled at assessing the treasure, then the *Webster's* [of course] *New Dictionary of Synonyms* (1973) may help, although the *Webster's New World Dictionary* makes room for such work, too. "Proper words in proper places, make the true definition of a style," said Jonathan Swift.

Dictionaries of quotations (Bartlett's, Oxford, Penquin) are worth having—not to extract ornamental remarks in the manner of the speaker at the Kiwanis Club (avoid quotation books organized by topic: you want them by author), but to find the precise words within a more or less fuzzy memory: What exactly did Swift say? Lack of precision will place you with the Florida football player who recalled the Good Book on the eve of the Florida State game: "Do unto others what they would like to do unto you."

It's instructive to keep a personal book of quotations, containing economic ideas you think are expressed well. The thing is called a "commonplace book," not because it is cheezy but because in classical rhetoric the commonly shared materials of Invention were called *loci communes*, literally "the common places," or "usual topics," "*koinoi topoi*" in Greek. Well kept, such a book can be the writer's journal of which Mills spoke. Simon James published his for economics, as *A Dictionary of Economic Quotations* (1984), which contains much encouraging evidence that at any rate British economists know how to turn a phrase.

10. *Keep Your Spirits Up, Forge Ahead, and the Like*

Now start writing. Here I must become less helpful, not because I have been instructed to hold back the secrets of the guild but because creativity is scarce. Where exactly the next sentence comes from is not obvious. If it were obvious then novels and economics papers could be written by machine.

If you can't think of anything to say, you might well read more, calculate more, and in general research more. Most research, however, turns out to be irrelevant to the paper you finally write, which is another reason to mix writing with the researching. The writing forces you to ask questions of the facts that are strictly relevant. The next sentence will sometimes reveal that you didn't do all the right research. The guiding question in research (research is not the subject here, but I won't charge extra) is "So What?" Answer that question in every sentence and you will become a great scholar; answer it once a page in a ten-page paper and you'll write a good one.

If after all this, though, you still have nothing to say, then perhaps your mind is poorly stocked with ideas in general. The solution is straightforward. Educate yourself. That is, live a life of wide experience, and spend big chunks of it reading the best our civilization has to offer, beginning tonight to learn elementary Greek. It's not too late to join the conversation:

> As civilized human beings, we are the inheritors, neither of an inquiry about ourselves and the world, nor of an accumulating body of information, but of a conversation begun in the primeval forest and extended and made more articulate in the course of centuries. . . . Education, properly speaking, is an initiation . . . in which we acquire the intellectual and moral habits appropriate to conversation. (Oakeshott, 1933, pp. 198–199).

Anyway, say it. Saying it out loud will help. If people wrote more like the way they spoke their writing would have more vigor (and if they spoke more like the way they wrote their speaking would have more precision). Writing expresses personality, as does the voice: it is said that to write well you need only to become good, and then write naturally. We are good when speaking to Mom or to a friend. We write well to them.

You hear a sentence when you read it out loud. It's a good rule to not write anything you would be embarrassed to speak out to the intended audience. Don't write entirely silently, or you will write entirely stiffly. Good modern prose has the rhythms of actual speech—intelligent and honest actual speech, that is to say, not the empty chatter of the sophomore trying to make it at the fraternity party or the waffling obscurity of the Labor Department bureaucrat trying to lie about black teenage unemployment. We exaggerate the power of words to conceal a shameful intent; generally the words expose it.

Regard the outline as an aid, not a master. When you get stuck, as you will, look at the outline, revise it, reread what you have written, reread the last bit out loud, talk to yourself about where it is going, imagine explaining it to a friend, try to imitate some way of speaking that Dennis or Maynard had, write a sentence parallel to the one just written, fill out the idea.

Don't panic if the words don't come; don't quit easily. Try changing the surroundings. Move to the library, sharpen a pencil, visit the fridge, block out noise with the earmuffs that ground personnel in airports wear, put classical music in your stereo (Bach is best for thinking, it has been shown; there is considerable doubt concerning Heavy Metal). Then get back to work. Don't expect to write easily all the time. Nobody does. Writing, like any form of thinking, flares and fizzles like a fire. Don't break off when on a burn. When writing well don't let anyone entice you into watching a movie on TV; tell Freddy to go away; resist breaking for a snack. Be selfish about your little candle of creation.

Keep the finished manuscript in some form handy for rereading and revising. A looseleaf ringbinder is good because it can be added to easily and is hard to misplace even on a

crowded desk. Replace the written manuscript in the binder
with a typed one and keep working on it. Print out preliminary
versions frequently from your computer and read the printout
critically. Richard Lanham has some good advice:

> The typewriter distances prose and it does it quickly. By deper-
> sonalizing our priceless prose, a typescript shows it to us as seen
> through a stranger's eyes. . . . No single bad writing habit is so
> powerful as the habit of typing an essay only when you are ready to
> turn it in. Correct the handwritten manuscript by all means, but
> then type a draft and revise that. (1979, p. 54).

When dull, and especially when starting a session, reread a big
chunk of the draft, pencil in hand (now more definitely a
pencil, or a pen of another color if a typist is involved) to
insert, amend, revise, correct, cancel, delete, and improve.
On a computer, scroll up to the beginning and read what
you've done like a reader, noting where your pace is checked
by some difficulty of expression.

At the end of a session, or at any substantial break, always
write down your thoughts, however vague, on what will come
next. Don't get up without doing this, even to answer nature's
call. Write or type the notes directly onto the end of the text,
where they can be looked at and crossed off as used. A few
scraps will do, and will save half an hour of warming up when
you start again. Jean Piaget, a titan of psychology—not, it
must be admitted, much of a stylist, but the matter here is
mere fluency—remarked once (1980, p. 1), "It's better to stop
in the middle of the sentence. Then you don't waste time
starting up." Paul Halmos urges the mathematical writer to
plan the next session at the end of the present one (1973, p.
28). After a session of writing the ideas not yet used stand ready
in the mind, and one should get them onto that ideal storage
medium, the piece of paper.

So much can be said about getting a first draft, and about
Invention and Arrangement.

11. *Speak to an Audience of Human Beings*

But Style, to repeat, is rewriting, and rewriting can be learned
in subrules. Rewriting can be tiresome. The myth of the free

lunch to the contrary, good or even adequate writing is easy for few writers, and some of the best work at it the hardest, working to make less work for the reader. Hemingway said, "Easy writing makes hard reading." Balzac rewrote his novels from printer's proofs as often as twenty-seven times, bankrupting himself with the expense [Lucas, 1955 (1974), p. 270]. Virginia Woolf rewrote parts of *The Waves* twenty times. Writing well takes as much devotion as playing an instrument well. The great violinist Giardini was asked how long it took him to learn how to play: "Twelve hours a day for twenty years" (p. 271).

Yet in truth the practice hours are not as stressful as the performances. Once you are equipped with a technique for doing it well much of the rewriting is pleasant and not excessively hard. Rewriting for Style does not at least have the anxiety of Invention and Arrangement, the anxiety that you will not be able to produce anything at all.

The first of the subrules of Style at the level of the essay as a whole is to look your audience directly in the eyes. Be honest with them. Ask who they are, aim the draft toward them, and keep hauling yourself back to facing them in revisions.

Choose a reader and stick with him. Changing your implied reader is in an economic sense inefficient. There is no point at all in telling your reader in a paper on the oil industry that oil is a black, burnable fluid, then turning to an exposition that assumes the reader understands supply and demand curves. If you've started with a preschooler for an implied reader you have to keep him around. Similarly, an article using the translog production function wastes motion if it rederives the elementary properties of a Cobb-Douglas production function. No one who has gotten so far into such an article will be innocent of Cobb-Douglas. The writing mixes up two mutually exclusive audiences.

The rule, then, is to choose someone to write for. Some find it best to choose an Implied Reader of imagination, an ideal economist; others find it best to choose a real person, such as Charles Kindleberger or good old Professor Smith or the friend down the hall. It is healthy discipline to be haunted by people with high standards, but with some sympathy for the enterprise, looking over your shoulder in imagination. It keeps the prose steady at one level of difficulty to imagine one master spirit.

The choice of audience determines who you are going to be in the essay, what rhetorical stance or authorial persona you are going to adopt: the Enthusiastic Student, the Earnest Scientist, the Reasonable and Modest Journeyman, the Genius, the Math Jock, the Professor, the Breezy Journalist. Look at a piece of economics and ask what Implied Author and Implied Reader it has in mind. The successful piece will have a reader you can be and an author you can tolerate. Writing is a little drama in which the writer chooses the roles. You cannot abstain as a writer from making a choice. Attempting to abstain leaves you choosing unthinkingly.

12. *Avoid Boilerplate*

A related piece of advice is that the writing must be interesting. This sounds harshly difficult. Few of us are great wits, and we know we aren't. But you can avoid some dullnesses by rule. Choosing oneself as the audience tends to dullness, since most of us admire uncritically even dull products of our own brains. A reasonably correct recitation of the history of prices and interest rates over the past ten years may strike its author as a remarkable intellectual achievement, filled with drama and novelty. But Charles Kindleberger, who wrote it, or good old Professor Smith, who lived it, or the colleague down the hall, who read it, probably don't agree. Spare them. Restatements of the well known bore the readers; routine mathematical passages bore the readers; excessive introduction and summarization bore the readers. Get to the point that sceptical but serious readers care about and stick to it.

Therefore, avoid boilerplate. Boilerplate in prose is all that is prefabricated and predictable. It is common in economic prose. Excessive introduction and summarizing is boilerplate. Other slabs of boilerplate are the redoings for a large number of repetitive cases what can be done just as well with a single well-chosen one. The academic pose inspires boilerplate. Little is getting accomplished with econometric chatter copied out of the textbook, rederivations of the necessary conditions for consumer equilibrium, and repetition of hackneyed formulations of the theory. Explaining a model of efficient capital markets by writing for the thousandth time "P_t given I_t, where I_t is all the information" does not advance understanding. If it didn't much help make Eugene Fama's work clear when he first uttered it, why suppose it will enlighten someone now?

Impenetrable theoretical remarks have great prestige in economics. A young writer of economics will sacrifice any amount of relevance and clarity to show that he can speak this way, too. The result is filigreed boilerplate. The economist will write about the completeness of arbitrage in this way: "Consider two cities, A and B, trading an asset, X. If the prices of X are the same in market A and in market B, then arbitrage may be said to be complete." The clear way to do this does not draw attention to its "theoretical" character at all: "New York and London in 1870 both had markets for Union Pacific bonds. The question is, did the bonds sell for the same in both places?"

The beginning often has boilerplate. Never start a paper with that universal hook of the bankrupt imagination, "This paper. . . ." Describing the art of the hook in the brief review, Jacques Barzun and Henry Graff note (1970, p. 272) that "the opening statement takes the reader from where he presumably stands in point of knowledge and brings him to the book under review." "This paper" does not take the reader anywhere (so never start a book review with "This book. . . ."). A paper showing that monopoly greatly reduces income might best start:

> Every economist knows by now that monopoly does not much reduce income [which is where he presumably stands in point of knowledge]. Every economist appears to be mistaken [thus bringing him to the matter under review].

It bores the reader to begin *"This paper* discusses the evidence for a large effect of monopoly on income." The reader's impulse, probably justified by the tiresome stuff to follow, is to give up.

Another piece of boilerplate attached to the early parts of

most student papers is "background." This is a polite word for padding, the material you collected that you later discovered was beside the point. It seems a shame not to use it, you say; and after all it gives the thing weight. Resist. If you have read a lot and if you have been thinking through the question you began with, asking and answering one question after another, you will have plenty to say. If you haven't read a lot and did not think through the questions you are asking, you will have nothing to say. No one will be fooled. You might as well save a tree.

Still another piece of beginning boilerplate, and one that kills the momentum of most papers in economics on the second page, is the table-of-contents paragraph: "The outline of this paper is as follows." Don't, for God's sake, don't. Nine out of ten readers skip to the substance, if they can find it; but the few who pause on the paragraph are wasting their time. They cannot understand it. Usually it has been written with no particular audience in mind, least of all the audience of first-time readers of the paper. Even when done well, which it seldom is, the table-of-contents paragraph lacks a purpose. You will practically never see it in good writing unless inserted by an editor who doesn't know good writing from bad. Weak writers defend it as a "roadmap." They got the idea from Miss Jones: "Tell the reader what you're going to say. Say it. Say that you've said it." It's exceptionally bad advice. The person who made up this memorable phrasing of it should be jailed at hard labor.

Therefore, avoid overtures, and do not give elaborate summaries of what you have said. Never repeat without apologizing for it ("as I said earlier"; or merely "again"). Unless you apologize the reader thinks you have not noticed the repetition, and will suspect that you have not thought through the organization. He'll be right. Remember, the paper that took you a week to write will be read in about half an hour. You must read the paper yourself in this rapid way to get the experience the reader will have, and to make the experience good.

The writer who wishes to be clear does not clot his prose with traffic directions. He thinks hard about the arrangement.

Add headings afterwards if you wish, especially ones with declarative sentences advancing the argument, like the ones used here. Your prose, however, should read well and clearly without the headings.

13. *Control Your Tone*

The tone of the writing and much of its clarity depends on choosing and then keeping an appropriate implied author, the character you pretend to be while writing. Again there is no escape from choice. You can't in particular just "be yourself," though you will probably do a more persuasive job if the implied author in your writing is similar to yourself. Writing, like teaching or social life, is a performance, a job of acting.

Everyone has a problem with tone, student or professor. The student will sometimes use an implied author encountered only in government forms, using phrases like "due to" and "period of time" and "views were opposing." No one really talks like this. Taking on the implied author Newspaper Reporter is a natural alternative, since much of the reading a student does is from newspapers. The stuff will be snappy, but it's hard to tolerate outside the newspaper. The journalist writes for the one-paragraph jolt. A Hollywood autobiography ("with the assistance of Elmer Snerd") will have this implied author. It reads like a year's worth of the *National Inquirer*.

Out of stage fright, professors in economics overuse the pompous and unintelligible implied author The Scientist. Have pity on them, and help them overcome their fear. C. Wright Mills's discussion of the problem of writing sociology is applicable to economics and other academic writing:

> Such lack of ready intelligibility, I believe, usually has little or nothing to do with the complexity of subject matter, and nothing at all with profundity of thought. It has to do almost entirely with certain confusions of the academic writer about his own status. . . . [Because the academic writer in America] feels his own lack of public position, he often puts the claim for his own status before his claim for the attention of the reader to what he is saying. . . . Desire for status is one reason why academic men [and women: Mills lived in a notably sexist age] slip so readily into unintelligi-

bility. . . . To overcome the academic *prose* you have first to overcome the academic *pose*. It is much less important to study grammar and Anglo-Saxon roots than to clarify your answer to these important questions: (1) How difficult and complex after all is my subject? (2) When I write, what status am I claiming for myself? (3) For whom am I trying to write? (1959, p. 218f)

In other words, it is lack of confidence that spoils academic writing.

The obscurity comes from hiding behind The Scientist. The pose of This-Stuff-Is-So-Complex-That-I-Can't-Be-Clear is usually strained when not an outright lie. It's really not that difficult to explain a Malthusian demographic model or a rational expectations model in plain words to smart people willing to pay attention. A reader of a student paper or of a professional journal is smart and willing. In other words, one must decide to be understood and worry some other time about being admired. Do not try to impress people who already understand the argument (they will not be amused). Try to explain in a personable tone to people who do not now understand.

Tone of writing is like tone of voice. It is personality expressed in prose. Students would do better to reveal more of their character in their writing. The college teacher mainly likes students (or else she would be selling insurance). So don't worry. Be charming, not servile or pompous. Similar words of comfort apply to the professor herself: relax; take off the mask of The Scientist.

The worst mistake is to be unpleasant: if you yell at people they will walk away, in reading as at a party. Avoid invective. "This is pure nonsense," "there is absolutely no evidence for this view," "the hypothesis is fanciful" are fun phrases to write, deeply satisfying as only political and intellectual passion can be, but they arouse the suspicion in any but the most uncritical audience that the argument needs a tone of passion to overcome its weakness.

Tone is transmitted by adverbs and adjectives. To mention the worst, run your pen through each "very" (or tell your word processor to flag it). Most things aren't very. "Absolutely," "pure," and the like are the same: most things aren't absolute or pure, and to claim so conveys a falsely emphatic tone. Even if you are in fact dogmatic and intolerant it will be less wearisome for the reader if you let some doubt enter your way of speaking. Screaming is not speaking well.

It has been said (Strunk and White, 1959) that "to air one's views gratuitously . . . is to imply that the demand for them is brisk" (p. 66). To air them intemperately reduces whatever demand there is. A comical example of what can go wrong with verbal abuse is: "These very tendentious arguments are false." The writer meant "tenuous" (look it up). But even had he said "tenuous," the word "these" gives the reader the fleeting and hilarious impression that the writer was characterizing his own arguments, not his victim's. Tendentious they are.

Wit compensates for tendentiousness, as is plain in the literary careers of the journalist H. L. Mencken and the economist George Stigler. Mencken's railings against the boobocracy, or Stigler's against the bureaucracy, are made less tiresome by rhetorical coyness, ducking behind self-repudiating exaggeration or arch understatement. Readers allow such writers more room to be opinionated because the opinions are so amusingly expressed.

Most academic prose, from both students and faculty, could use more humor. There is nothing unscientific in self-deprecating jokes about the sample size, and nothing unscholarly in dry wit about the failings of intellectual opponents. Even a pun can bring cheer to a grader working through the thirtieth paper. A writer must entertain if he is to be read. Only third-rate scholars and C− students are so worried about the Academic Pose that they insist on their dignity. The rich laboratory humor of economic science—Griliches's Law that more than five variables in a cross section yields garbage, for instance—should find its way into articles. Maybe it would drive out the tiresome witticisms about imaginary economic goods, commonly called "widgets."

The economist Robert Solow should be followed in this. He is aware of what he does, and how it contrasts with the usual denatured tone of articles in economics:

Personality is eliminated from journal articles because it's felt to be 'unscientific.' An author is proposing a hypothesis, testing a hypothesis, proving a theorem, not persuading the reader that this is a better way of thinking about X than that. Writing would be better if more of us saw economics as a way of organizing thoughts and perceptions about economic life rather than as a poor imitation of physics. (1984).

14. *Paragraphs Should Have Points*

So much for the essay. Turn then to the paragraph. The paragraph should be a more or less complete discussion of one topic. Paragraphing is punctuation, similar to stanzas in poetry. The stanzas cannot be too long. You will want occasionally to pause for various reasons, having completed a bit of discussion, shifting the tone perhaps or simply giving the reader a break. The reader will skip around when his attention wanders, and naturally skips to the next paragraph. If your paragraphs are too long (as they will tend to be from a word processor, by the way) the reader will skip a lot of your stuff to get to the next break.

Paragraphs, though, should not be too short too often.

The same is true of sentences.

Short paragraphs give a breathless quality to the writing.

Newspaper writers, especially on the sports page, often write in one-sentence paragraphs, for the sheer excitement of it.

Big quotations (in a block if more than eight typed lines, with no quotation marks) have two legitimate jobs. First, they can give the devil his due. If you plan to rip to pieces a particular argument then you must quote it in full, to give at least the impression of being fair. Mild criticism, however, cannot follow a big quote: you must indeed rip it to pieces, word by word. Otherwise the reader feels that the effort of settling into a new style has not been worthwhile. Second, block quotations can give an angel his voice. If Armen Alchian said something strikingly well with which you entirely agree then you do not hurt your case by repeating what he said, and gain from his authority. Routine explanations do not belong anywhere, whether in long or short quotations. They convey the impression that you think with your scissors, and not very well at that.

(Another parenthetical word is in order here, this time about plagiarism. For someone who has gotten this far it's probably unnecessary. "Plagiarism" is using other people's sentences with the intent of claiming them as your own. The worst students sometimes do it out of desperation, then claim that they didn't understand. Because they are the worst students they often get caught, which is sad. It is a serious offense, grounds for expulsion. No college paper can be fashioned by stringing together passages from other writers. Your teachers know you can read, at least in the sense of spelling out the words: they want you to learn how to think and to write.)

15. *Make Tables, Graphs, and Displayed Equations Readable*

The wretched condition of tables and graphs in economics shows how small is the economist's investment in expression. The main point is that tables and graphs are writing, and the usual rules of writing therefore apply. Bear your audience in mind. Try to be clear. Be brief. Ask: "Is this entry necessary? Would I dribble on in a similar way in prose or mathematics?" No reader wishes to have the annual figures of income between 1900 and 1980 when the issue in question is the growth of income over the whole span. The reader wants statistics given in the simplest form consistent with their use. The eight digits generated by the average calculator are not ordinarily of any use. The elasticity is about 3-1/7 not 3.14159256.*

Titles and headings in tables should be as close to self-explanatory as possible, a rule that guides some book publishers and should guide more journal publishers. In headings of tables you should use words, not computer acronyms. Remember: you're trying to be clear, not Scientific. A column labeled "LPDOM" requires a step of translation to get to the meaning: "Logarithm of the Domestic Price." You want people to understand your stuff, not to jump through mental hoops.

The same principles should guide graphs and diagrams.

---

* The point is widely misunderstood. Read Oskar Morgenstern, *On the Accuracy of Economic Observations* (2nd ed.), Chapter 1.

Edward R. Tufte's fine book, *The Visual Display of Quantitative Information* (1983), demonstrates such precepts as "Mobilize every graphical element, perhaps several times over, to show the data" (p. 139; Tufte is not to be taken as a guide to writing prose). Use titles for diagrams and for tables that state their theme, such as "All Conferences Should Happen in the Midwest" instead of "A Model of Transport Costs." Use meaningful names for lines, points, and areas, not alphanumeric monstrosities: "Rich Budget Line" instead of "Locus QuERtY." You'll find it easier to follow your own logic.

The same things can be said of displayed equations. It is much clearer to say "the regression was Quantity of Grain = 3.56 + 5.6 (Price of Grain) − 3.8 (Real Income)," than "the regression was $Q = 3.56 + 5.6P − 3.8Y$, where Q is quantity of grain, P its price, and Y real income." Anyone can retrieve the algebra from the words, but the reverse is pointlessly harder. The retrieval is hard even for professional mathematicians. The set theorist Halmos said: "The author had to code his thought in [symbols] (*I deny that anybody thinks in [such] terms*), and the reader has to decode" (1973, p. 38, italics mine). Stanislaw Ulam, with many other mathematicians, complains of the raising of the symbolic ante in recent years: "I am turned off when I see only formulas and symbols, and little text. It is too laborious for me to look at such pages not knowing what to concentrate on" (1976, p. 275f). Tables, graphs, diagrams, and displayed equations should elucidate the argument, not obscure it.

16. *Footnotes Are Nests for Pedants*

A footnote should be subordinate. That is why it is at the foot of the page. In academic and student writing, however, the most important work often gets done in the small print at the bottom of the page. The best sustained example in economics is Schumpeter's *History of Economic Analysis*, in which the liveliest prose and the strongest points occur toward the end of footnotes spilling over three pages. Footnotes should not be used as a substitute for good arrangement. If the idea does not fit maybe it does not belong. Cluttering the main text with

little side trips will break up the flow of ideas, like the footnote*
attached to this sentence.

Footnotes should guide the reader to the sources. That is all.
When they strain to do something else something goes wrong.
It is dangerous to use footnotes and other citations to display
what you don't have. The attempt to assume the mantle of The
Scholar looks foolish when the best one can do is cite the
textbook. Citing whole books and articles is a contagion in
modern economics, spread by the author-date citation, such as
that used by this book. It is easier for the author to write "See
The General Theory" than to bother to find the page and
sentence where Keynes, fatally, adopts the mistaken assump-
tion of a closed economy. By not bothering to find it the author
misses the chance to really know whether Keynes did.

17. *Make Your Writing Cohere*

Behind such rules on what to avoid in slugs of prose in tables,
graphs, footnotes, and paragraphs lies a rule on what to seek. It
is the Rule of Coherence: make writing hang together. The
reader can understand things in phrase or paragraph or book
that hang together. He cannot understand things filled with
irrelevancies.

Look again at the paragraph I just wrote. It is no masterpiece, but you probably grasped it without much effort. The
reason you did is that each sentence is linked to the previous
one. The first promises a "rule." The second names it, repeating the word "rule"; after the colon the next bit delivers on the
promise of the name, using the phrase "hang together." The
next tells why it is a good rule, reusing "hang together" and
introducing a character called "the reader," saying that he "can
understand" certain "things." The final sentence emphasizes
the point by putting it the other way, saying what *things he* [the

---

* Inviting the reader to look away is not wise. Practically never is it a good idea
to do what this note does, breaking a sentence. It should have been woven
into the text, if it said anything, which it does not. An amusing footnote on
the matter, viewing it more cheerfully, is G. W. Bowersock, "The Art of the
Footnote" (1983/1984).

same] *cannot understand*. The paragraph itself hangs together and is easily grasped by the mind.

Its structure is (AB) (BC) (CD). Note the linkages of repetition, one B connected with another, C with C, and so forth. Economists would call it "transitive" writing. To do it you must violate the schoolmarm's rule of not repeating words. Verily, you *must* repeat them, linking the sentences and using pronouns like "it" or "them" to relieve monotony. The linkages can be tied neatly, if not too often, by repeating words with the same root in different versions, as was just done with the verb "linking" in the previous sentence and the noun "linkages" in this (the figure is called in classical rhetoric "polyptoton"). There are other tricks of cohesion. They rely on repetition. (In this paragraph for instance the word "repetition" is repeated right to the end in various forms: repetition, repeating, repeat, repeating, repetition.)

If you draw on the tricks you will be less likely to fill your prose with irrelevancies: (AB) (BC) (CD) looks pretty, is easy to understand, and is probably reasonable; (ABZYX) (MNOP) (BJKLC) looks ugly, is impossible to understand, and is probably nonsense. A newspaper editor once gave this advice to a cub reporter: "It doesn't much matter what your first sentence is. It doesn't even much matter what the second is. But the third damn well better follow from the first and second." If you once start a way of talking—a metaphor of birth or a tone of patient explanation—you have to carry through, making the third sentence follow from the others. You must reread what you have written again and again, unifying the tenses of the verbs, unifying the vocabulary, unifying the form. That's how to get unified, transitive paragraphs.

Yet, a clumsy way to get transitive paragraphs begins each sentence with a linking word. Indeed, not only did good Latin prose in the age of Cicero have this feature, but also Greek had it, even in common speech. In English, however, it is not successful. Therefore, many Ciceronian and Greek adverbs and conjunctions are untranslatable. To be sure, the impulse to coherence is commendable. But on the other hand (as must be getting clear by now), you tire of being pushed around by the writer, told when you are to take a sentence illustratively ("indeed"), adversatively ("however," "but"), sequentially ("furthermore," "therefore"), or concessively ("to be sure"). You are bumped by clanking machinery, the "not only . . . but also." Machinery of outlining and summarizing has similar results. It is not the genius of English. English achieves coherence by repetition, not by signal. Repeat, and your paragraphs will cohere.

18. *Use Your Ear*

Prose has rhythms, some better than others. Thomas Babbington Macaulay and Martin Luther King knew rhythm in speech. Someone less gifted can at least avoid the ugliest ones, by listening to what they have written. For instance, if every sentence is of the same length and construction, the paragraph will become monotonous. If you have some dramatic reason for repeating the construction, the repetition is good. If you have no good reason for doing so, the reader will feel misled. If you talk always in sentences of precut form, the paragraph will have a monotonous rhythm. If you have been paying attention recently, you will see what I mean.

The novelist John Gardner gave some advice on the variety of sentences (1983, p. 104f). Become self-conscious, he said, about how much you're putting into each part. An English sentence has three parts: subject, verb, object. Thus: subject = "an English sentence"; verb = "has grammatically speaking" ("grammatically speaking" modifies the verb); object = "three parts: subject, verb, object." Vary your sentences by how much you put into each. In the sentence just finished the score is: subject absent but understood = "you"; verb = "vary," complexly modified by "how much you put into each"; object = "your sentences," quite simple, though not as simple as the subject. Gardner, who wrote rather well, uncovered beautifully with his simple principle of the three sentence parts that we have just discussed and could discuss more if it were a good idea, which it is not, because we've said enough already, the graceless rhythm that results from an overburdened sentence such as this one, in which every part has much too much in it, every phrase too much in the way of adjectives and adverbs modifying its elements, which exhausts the reader, and confuses her. Notice that you stopped paying attention about half way through it. A sentence with too much in it can ruin a whole paragraph.

19. *Write in Complete Sentences*

Which leads to the sentence. That is not one. Such tricks should be attempted only occasionally, and only for a reason (here: a dramatic surprise, if corny). Write mainly in complete sentences. This isn't a matter of school grammar. It's a matter of not raising expectations that you don't fulfill. As a fluent speaker of English (or at least of your dialect), you can know when a sentence is a sentence by asking whether it could stand as an isolated remark. Now the phrase "As a fluent speaker of English" could stand alone, but only as an answer to a question in a conversation. Socrates: "Tell me, Polus: how do you know what a sentence is?" Polus: "As a fluent speaker of English." Ask if it could stand alone as an isolated remark. No, it can't. If someone came up to you on the street and said "As a fluent speaker of English," you would expect him to continue. If, staring at you fixedly with a maniacal smile, he did not, you would edge carefully away.

20. *Avoid Elegant Variation*

The first duty in writing a sentence is to make it clear. A way to make it clear is to use one word to mean one thing. Get your words and things lined up and keep them that way. The positive rule is Strunk and White's: "Express parallel ideas in parallel form." (An example will be given in the next sentence.) The negative rule is Fowler's: "Avoid Elegant Variation." I've just done the parallel trick. The two ideas are parallel and are expressed in parallel form: *"The positive rule is* Strunk and White's" leads my reader to expect *"The negative rule is* Fowler's." One expects the pair "positive" and "negative." The reader gets what he expects. He can fit the little novelties into what he already knows.

Elegant Variation uses many words to mean one thing, with

the result that in the end no reader, and certainly not the writer, knows what the thing is. A paper on economic development used in two pages all these: "industrialization," "growing structural differentiation," "economic and social development," "social and economic development," "development," "economic growth," "growth," and "revolutionized means of production." With some effort you can see in context that they all mean about the same thing. The writer simply liked the sound of the differences, and had studied elegance too young. A writer on economic history wrote about the "indifferent harvests of 1815 [bad crops] and calamitous volume deficiencies of 1816 [very bad crops]." It takes a while to see that both mean the same thing, a pretty simple thing. Notice that in these cases, as commonly, the Elegant Variation comes draped in five-dollar words ("growing structural differentiation" = new jobs in manufacturing; "calamitous volume deficiencies" = very bad crops).

Some people who write this way mistake the purpose of writing, believing it to be an occasion for empty display. The eighth grade, they should realize, is over. Most people do it out of correctable ignorance, as in: "the new economic history is concerned not only with what happened but also with why events turned out as they did." Something is wrong. The logic is that the reader imagines fleetingly that "what happened" and the "events [that] turned out as they did" are different things. He must give thought to whether they are. This is what is wrong with Elegant Variation. It requires thought, the pointless thought required to see that calamitous volume deficiencies are the same thing as very bad crops. It wastes the reader's attention on unimportant matters. If the reader's attention strays a little—and it is always straying, a lot—he will come away from the sentence without knowing what it said.

21. *Watch How Each Word Connects with Others*

Trimming away the elegant variation, like other rules of rewriting, does not make the writer's life easy. Most people's first drafts are jammed with elegant variation, traffic signals, illogical sentences, nonsentences, misquotations, boilerplate, monotonies, and jingles. Easy writing, remember, makes hard reading. Johnson said, "What is written without effort is in general read without pleasure." Like effort in any work, such as sewing or auto repair, you must check and tighten, check and tighten. In short sessions the exercise will please you. It is good to do something well. The neat seam in a dress or the smooth joint in a fender revive the spirit worn from the effort. Still, before the end it is tiring and the result will seem too obvious. Do nouns and verbs link successive sentences? Have I used one word to mean one thing? Have I used parallel forms to emphasize parallel ideas? Can I drop any word? Check and tighten.

The care extends to tiny details. For instance, you must choose repeatedly whether to carry over words from one construction to its parallel. It's either "the beautiful and *the* damned" or "the beautiful and damned." Such choices will occur scores of times in a paper. F. Scott Fitzgerald, seeking elegant variation, could have entitled his book *The Beautiful Folks and Those People Who Are Damned*, in which case the choice would not have been posed. No one would have heard of F. Scott Fitzgerald.

Other tools to line up word and thing are singulars and plurals, masculines and feminines. Unlike the inflected Latin and Anglo-Saxon from which it descends, English does not hitch related words by case and gender (surviving in he, she, it, her, him, his, hers, its, I, me, my). Use the few resources we have. The following sentence, for example, is ambiguous because "them" can refer to so many things: "*Owners* of the original and indestructible powers of the soil earned from *them* [powers or owners?] pure rents, and that tenant farmers were willing to pay *them* [the rents? the owners? the powers?] indicates that these powers of the soil were useful." You can work out what it means, but remember that the object is not to write so the reader can understand but so he cannot possibly misunderstand. The singular and plurals here are not essential to the meaning, and so they can be exploited to make it clear: "*An owner* of the original and indestructible powers of the soil earned from *them* [now effortlessly unambiguous because it agrees with the only plural referent available: the powers] pure rents, and that the tenant farmers were willing to pay *him* [unambiguous: the owner] indicates that these powers of the soil were useful." The use of "she" alongside "he" can in like fashion become an advantage for clarity of reference as much as a blow for sexual equality. If you assign gender to the two people you are talking about then suddenly he will see what you mean.

Capitals are useful word-changes, too: you can make a word into a concrete and Proper Noun by capitalizing it, which is useful for reference. It's easy to point at a named Thing. That's why arguments in economics go by names, even by names of people: "the Coase Theorem" is more vivid than "the proposition that property rights matter to allocation in the case of high transaction costs." Capitalization can be used nicely for referring to a Point in a diagram. Be careful, though: capitals have an Ironic Air to them, which is fun only in moderation (I tend to use them Too Much).

22. *Watch Punctuation, Weeding Out Excess Commas*

Another detail is punctuation. You might think it would be easy, since there are only seven marks (excepting parentheses [and brackets, which are used in the style of math for parentheses within parentheses or for your insertions into someone else's words]). But feelings run strong on the matter. Never use the exclamation point! Well, hardly ever! It is hysterical! The period is no problem, though to understand the most notable use of it in literature you have to know that in the English of England it is called a "full stop": in the last sentence of their spoof history of England, *1066 and All That*, Sellars and Yeatman write that after the First World War "America became Top Nation and history came to a." Nor is the question mark a problem: judge it by ear; are you using the questioning tone of voice? The dash—used like this, a sort of parenthesis spoken in a louder tone of voice—can be overused to solve a problem with a badly organized sentence too easily, but is not otherwise difficult.

A lot of people are confused about the colon (:) and the semicolon (;). The safest rule is that the colon indicates an illustration to follow: just like this. The semicolon indicates a parallel remark; it is (as here) an additional illustration. It is also used to mark off items in series when the items themselves are long. "Faith, hope, and charity" uses commas; but if each item were elaborated ("Charity, the greatest of these, the light of the world;" and similarly with each) you might use the semicolon (;) as a sort of supercomma. You can see that the semicolon is also a sort of subperiod; you can hurry the pace a bit by splicing two sentences with a semicolon, as here. So the semicolon falls between comma and period. Remember the difference between colon and semicolon by noting that the semicolon contains both a comma and a period within it, a printed compromise.

Weak writers these days use too many commas and use them by rule rather than by ear, probably because Miss Jones told them to. It's no rule of life for instance that "an if-clause always requires a comma after it" or "When a clause cannot stand alone it must be hedged with commas." In fact, such rules lead to a comma in nearly every sentence and a consequent slowing of pace. When applied too enthusiastically a rule-driven comma ends up separating subject from verb. (Notice that I did use a comma after the "In fact" in the sentence before last but not after "When applied too enthusiastically" in the next. Stay tuned.) In revision the trick is to delete most commas before "the," as I just did after "In revision," and did a couple of sentences earlier after "When applied too enthusiastically"; I don't do it after "In fact" in the earlier sentence because the next word was not "the." The "the" signals a new phrase well enough without the clunk of a comma.

And yet . . . and yet: one must not be overemphatic. It is easy to fall into silly rules for commas, mine as well as thine. The best general rule is to punctuate by ear rather than by rule, and to insert a comma, as after "rule" here, where the pause in speaking seems to want it or where you as a reader get lost without it. When you want your prose to be read slowly and deliberately, and you have signaled this academic tone in other ways as well, then use commas heavily. For most writing use them lightly.

23. *Switch Around the Order Until It Sounds Good*

The inflected languages have more freedom of order than English. In Latin *Homo canem mordet* means the same thing as *Canem mordet homo*, with only a difference of emphasis; but "man bites dog" and "dog bites man" are news items of different orders. Still, much can be done with the order of an English sentence. With the order of an English sentence much can be done. You can do much with the order of an English sentence. It's mainly a matter of ear: proper words in proper places. Tinker with the sentence until it works.

A problem comes with modifiers, especially with adverbs, which float freely in English. The phrase "which is *again merely* another notation for. . . ." should be "which *again* is *merely* another notation for. . . ." Moving the "again" prevents it from piling up against the other modifier. Or: "the elasticities are *both with respect* to the price" should be "*both* elasticities are *with respect* to the price." Until they work, try out the words in various places. In various places try out the words until they work. Try out the words in various places until they work. There. If you can't get them to work, give up the sentence as a bad idea.

You should cultivate the habit of mentally rearranging the order of words and phrases of every sentence you write. Rules, as usual, govern the rewriting. One rule of arrangement is to avoid breaking, as in this clause, the flow with parenthetical remarks. Put the remark at the end if it's important and at the beginning if it's not.

The most important rule of rearrangement is that the end of the sentence is the place of emphasis. I wrote the sentence first as ". . . is the emphatic *location*," which put the emphasis on the word "location." The reader leaves the sentence with the last word ringing in her ears. I wanted, however, to emphasize the idea of emphasis, not the idea of location. So I rewrote it as ". . . is the place of *emphasis*." You should examine every sentence to see whether the main idea comes at the end—or, secondarily, the beginning. Dump less important things in the middle, or in the trash. A corollary of the rule is that putting less important things at the end will weaken the sentence. It would be grammatical to write ". . . that putting trivial things at the end will weaken the sentence *is a corollary of the rule*." Yet it shifts the emphasis to something already finished, *the rule*. The clearer way puts the emphasis on the novelty, the idea of the weakened sentence, by putting it at the end.

Listen for sentences that are monotonously long or short; listen for straggling sentences, as from

> That foolish young man of Japan,
> Whose limericks never would scan.
> When asked why it was
> He replied, "It's because
> I always try to get as much into the very last line as I ever
>   possibly can.

Adding one more idea at the last minute causes straggling, which comes even in a perfectly grammatical sentence like the present, making the sentence hard to read, which will cause the reader to stop reading after he has tried a couple of sentences like this one, which straggle, straggle, straggle. Remember Gardner's rule of not complicating more than one of the triad subject, verb, object. The lengthy pieces, as I said, should be at the end, although the rule will often conflict with the rule of putting the important matter at the end. At a minimum you should be aware of length and try it out in different portions of the sentence. The success of those eighth-grade ornaments, the doublet and the triplet, depends critically on shifting the longest portions to the end: "Keynes and the Keynesians" works, "The Keynesians and Keynes" does not; "faith, hope, and charity" works, "charity, faith, and hope" does not.

24. *Read, Out Loud*

Reading out loud is a powerful technique of revision. By
reading out loud you hear your writing as others hear it
internally, and if your ear is good you'll detect bad parts. For
instance, it's practically impossible to decide when to use
contractions like "you'll" or "it's" in semiformal prose without
reading the sentence out loud. By reading out loud, furthermore, you'll pick up unintentional rhymes (at times your lines
will chime), which can be distracting and mirth-provoking.
The rule is this: do not write anything that you would be
embarrassed to speak out loud to the intended audience. As
usual, Hemingway had the word, although I am not to use
it in a family publication: "The writer needs a build-in,
shockproof _____ detector." You know more about good
taste in the language and how to spot _____ than you may
think. If in rereading your writing out loud you blush to hear
an over-fancy sentence or a jargony word, change it.

No one, though, knows everything just because he's an
English-speaking, free-born citizen of a republic. The ear is
trained by exercise. Read the best old books (only when books
are old do we know whether they are the best: the best-sellers of
today are mostly rubbish). Take pleasure in the language of
literature. Read poetry out loud, lots of it, the best. Memorize
some of it. If you stop reading good writing when you leave
school you will stop improving your ear. Even an economist's
ear should ring with our English literature. Close study of
Time and the *Wall Street Journal* does not normally suffice as
an education in literacy—although it must be admitted that
Meg Greenfield, Mike Royko, James Kilpatrick, George Will,
and William Safire use the newspaper language well, and are
good models. They got that way, though, by reading the real
stuff, Shakespeare and Ring Lardner.

25. *Use Verbs, Active Ones*

Finally, words. The snappiest rules of good writing are about
words. For instance: write with nouns and, especially, verbs,

not with adjectives and adverbs. In revision the adjectives and adverbs should be the first to go. Delete as many as you can. A century and a half ago Sydney Smith wrote, "In composing, as a general rule, run your pen through every other word you have written; you have no idea what vigour it will give to your style."

He might have followed his own advice more fully, and would have done so if writing nowadays:

> In composing [of course it's composing: that's what we're talking about], as a general rule [what would be the point of any other?], run your pen through every other word you have written [of course writing: again, that's what we're talking about; and in any case, what else would you run a pen through? Your finger?]; you have no idea what vigour it will give to your style [for God's sake, how often do you have to repeat that you are talking about style?].

The result is: "Run your pen through every other word; you have no idea what vigour it will give." (In both Smith's version and mine the word "it" is ambiguous; it's not instantly clear what "it" refers to; but that is another matter.)

Use active verbs: not "active verbs should be used," which is cowardice, hiding the user behind a screen. Rather: "you should use active verbs." The imperative is a good substitute for the passive, especially for taking a reader through mathematical arguments: "then divide both sides by x" instead of "both sides are then divided by x."

Verbs make English. If you pick out active, accurate, and lively verbs you will write in an active, accurate, and lively style. You should find the action in a sentence and express it in a verb. Expressing it in a phrase functioning as a noun saps vigor. The disease is called "nominalization," and it afflicts most academic prose (mine, for instance). Joseph Williams, who discusses it at length, gives an example that might have come from economics: "There is a data reanalysis need," in which the only verb is the colorless "is," and the real action is buried in the nouns "need" and "reanalysis" (1981, p. 12). You can fix such a sentence by using verbs: "We must reanalyze our data." Notice that a real verb requires a real subject. There's no place to hide. The "data reanalysis need," by contrast, merely exists, blessedly free from personal responsibility (the freedom

from responsibility makes nominalization popular among bureaucrats). The general rule is to circle every "is" and try to
denominalize the sentences containing them. Find the actor
and the action. Find the verb. Follow the general rule: delete
"is" when you can. You have no idea what vigor it will bring.

26. *Avoid Words That Bad Writers Love*

Because it is easy at the level of the single word to detect and
punish miscreants the legislative attitude towards prose reaches
its heaven in lists of Bad Words. Some perfectly good English
words have died this way; for instance, "ain't." Even good
writers have such lists, often sensible. At a minimum certain
words tag you as incompetent simply because good writers
have decided so. It's unfair to the inexperienced and there's
nothing in the nature of the linguistic universe to justify it, but
you might as well know for instance that in some company if
you use "hopefully" to mean "I hope" instead of "with hope"
you will be set down as a jerk. Hopefully General Booth
entered heaven.

If economic prose would drop "via," "the process of,"
"intra," "and/or," "hypothesize," "respectively," and (a strange
one, this) "this" the gain in clarity and grace would be
substantial. If economic prose would drop "at least minimal,"
"thus," "overall," "basic," and "factor" the world would be
saved. The best practice provides the standard. Virginia Woolf
would not write "and/or" (or "he/she") because she wanted
prose, not a diagram. Some others that I'm sure she would
have disliked appear in my personal list of Bad Words.

Bad Words

Vague nouns and pronouns

concept: a vague, latinate, front-parlor word; consider "idea,"
"notion," or "thought."

data: over- and misused in economics. "Data" are plural, although it is clearly on its way to becoming singular in the
language. "Data" means "givens" in Latin, and that is how you
should use it, not as a do-all synonym for "facts," "statistics,"
"information," "observations," and so forth. The word em-

bodies, incidentally, a dangerous attitude toward observation—
that it is "given" by someone else—but the point here is one of
style. "Datum" is one "data."

function: in the sense of "role" is Latinate.

situation: vague. "Position" or "condition" are better, depending
on the meaning.

individuals: for plain "people."

structure: vague. There are no obvious alternatives to "structure"
because the word usually doesn't mean anything. On this and
other similar ones in economics, see Fritz Machlup (1963
[1967]).

process: usually empty, and can be struck out (sometimes with its
"the") without changing the meaning: "the economic development process" or "the transition process" becomes plain "economic development" or "the transition."

the existence of: strike it out, and just name the thing.

time frame: means "time"; it originates in the engineer's dim
notion that "time" means "passage of time" alone, and not
segments of time. But the notion is false. "This point in time" is
the correlate phrase. Drop it.

Pretentious and feeble verbs

critique: Elegant variation for "criticize" or "to read critically" or
"to comment on."

implement: Washingtonese, a rich and foolish dialect of Econo-
mese.

comprise: Fancy talk for "include" or "consist of."

analyze: Over- and misused in economics as a synonym for
"discuss" or "examine." Look it up in your dictionary.

hypothesize: For "suppose" or "expect." This word tags you as
lacking taste (similar words: "finalize," "and/or," "time frame").

finalize: Boardroom talk. See "hypothesize," which is academic
boardroom talk.

state: in the sense of "say"; why not say "say"?

try and do something is "try to do something" (strangely, "try and"
is common among educated English people; in the United
States it is a marker of incompetence).

the reason was due to: try again.

Pointless adjectives

former . . . latter: "the above"; "the preceding"; and other words
that request the reader to look back to sort out the former and
latter things. Don't request the reader to look back, because he

will, and will lose his place. Never ask the reader to solve a
puzzle, because he won't be able to, and will get angry.

aforementioned: What are you writing, a will?

intra/inter: in coinages, do not use. Do not present verbal puzzles
to your reader. Everyone has to stop to figure out what these
prefixes mean. Use "within" and "between." "International"
and "intramural" are fine, of course, being well domesticated.
But "The inter- and intrafirm communication was weak" is
silly. Fancy talk.

interesting: A weak word, made weak by its common sarcastic use
and by its overuse by people with nothing to say about their
subject except that it is interesting. It arouses the reader's
sadism.

kind of, sort of, type of: vague, vague, vague. Use sparingly.

Useless adverbs

fortunately, interestingly, etc.: Cheap ways of introducing irrelevant opinion.

hopefully: A marker of poor taste when used to mean "I hope," as I
have noted.

respectively: as in "Consumption and investment were 90 percent and 10 percent of income, respectively." Why would
anyone reverse the correct order of the numbers? (Answer:
someone who doesn't express parallel ideas in parallel form.)
Drawing attention to the lack of parallelism by mentioning
explicitly that it did *not* take place is a bad idea. When the list is
longer, distribute the numbers directly; "Consumption was 85
percent of income, investment 10 percent, and government
spending 5 percent."

very: The very general rule is to think very hard before using
"very" very much, and to very often strike it out. It is a weak
word.

for convenience: As in, "For convenience, we will adopt the
following notation." An idiotic phrase, when you think about it.
All writing should be for convenience. What would be the point
of writing for inconvenience?

vis à vis: French meaning "face-to-face"; use it to mean this, not
"relative to" or something even more vague. I have seen it
spelled "viza vi"; someone was not using the dictionary.

Clumsy conjunctions

due to: usually signals a clumsy phrase, due to not arranging the
sentence to sound right.

via: plain "by" is the word wanted.
in terms of: clumsy and vague; cf. "due to."
thus and ***hence:*** use sparingly, for they are traffic signals.
plus to mean ***and:*** use "and" until the language has finished
  changing "plus" into "and," which will take another century or
  so. I know you use it when you talk: well, speech can be
  improved by writing, too.

Words are a problem in economics. The vocabulary of
economics, like other vocabularies, is enriched by coinages
and borrowings: the Laffer curve, the affluent society, the
agency problem. Contrary to a widespread impression among
noneconomists, though, mastering the vocabulary of economics is not the same as mastering economics.

Everyone, economist or not, comes equipped with a vocabulary for the economy. It might be called Ersatz Economics.
In Ersatz Economics, prices start by "skyrocketing." When
"sellers outnumber buyers" prices fall from "exorbitant" levels,
probably "gouging," down through "fair" and "just." If this
"vicious cycle" goes on too long, though, they fall to "unfair"
and "cutthroat," the result of "dumping." Likewise, the man in
the street believes he knows that unions and corporations have
more "bargaining power" than do their victims, and therefore
can "exploit" them. A consumer can "afford" medical care,
maybe only "barely afford" it, "needs" housing, and views food
as a "basic necessity." Businesspeople maintain their "profit
margins," probably "obscene" or "unwarranted," by "passing
along" a higher wage, which causes workers to demand still
higher wages, in a "spiral." The protection of the American
worker's "living wage" from "unfair competition" by "cheap
foreign labor" should be high on the nation's list of "priorities,"
as should be the "rebuilding" of our "collapsing" industrial
"base."

To write thoughtfully in economics you must clear your
mind of such cant, as to understand astronomy you must stop
talking about the sun "rising."

27. *Be Concrete*

The first general rule of words is Be Concrete. A singular word
is more concrete than a plural (compare "Singular words are

more concrete than plurals"). Definiteness is concrete. Prefer
Wonder Bread to bread, bread to widgets, and widgets to X.
Bad writers in economics sometimes use abstraction because
they have nothing to say and don't want the fact to become too
plain, in the style of educational bureaucrats. Mostly, though,
they use abstraction to get general. They do not believe that
the ordinary reader will understand that "Wonder Bread"
stands for any commodity or that "ships" stand for all capital.
Secret codes use the principle that translation is often easier in
one direction than the other. Contrary to what most economic
writers seem to think, a reader finds it harder to get abstractions
down into examples than to raise examples to abstractions.
Much economic writing reads like a code: "%&* marginal
¢¢¢$$processof &%$¢ß ¢$% !structure."

Professional economists develop into professional code
breakers. To an economist there does not seem to be much
wrong with a sentence such as this: "Had *capital and labor* in
1860 embodied the same *technology* used in 1780, the *increase
in capital* would barely have offset the fixity of land." There is
a better way: "Had the *machines and men* of 1860 embodied
the same *knowledge of how to spin cotton or move cargo* as in
1780, the *larger numbers of spindles and ships* would have
barely offset the fixity of land." In a paper on Australia the
phrase "sheep and wheat" would do just fine in place of
"natural resource-oriented exports." In a paper on economic
history "Spanish prices began to rise before the treasure came"
would do just fine in place of "the commencement of the
Spanish Price Revolution antedated the inflow of treasure."
Writing should make things clear, not put them into a code of
Latinate abstraction.

28. *Be Plain*

The encoding, as I said earlier, often uses five-dollar words to
support a pose of The Scientist or The Scholar. The pose is
pathetic: science and scholarship depend on the quality of
argument, not on the level of diction. "The integrative conse-
quences of growing structural differentiation" means in hu-
man-being talk "the need for others that someone feels when

he buys rather than bakes his bread." Anglo-Saxon words (need, someone, feels, buys, bakes, bread) have often acquired a homely concreteness through long use that more recent and more scholarly coinages from Latin or Greek have not (integrative, consequences, structural, differentiation: all directly from Latin, without even a domesticating sojourn in French). "Geographical and cultural factors function to spatially confine growth to specific regions for long periods of time" means in Anglo-Saxon and Norman French "It's a good bet that once a place gets poor it will stay poor."

Five-dollar words are not without their charm. In the hands of a master they transmit a splendid irony, as in the analysis of sports by the great American economist, Thorstein Veblen: sports "have the advantage that they afford a politely blameless outlet for energies that might otherwise not readily be diverted from some useful end." But you've got to be Thorstein Veblen to get away with such stuff. In most hands it's just Latin-fed, polysyllabic baloney: "Thus, it is suggested, a deeper understanding of the conditions affecting the speed and ultimate extent of an innovation's diffusion is to be obtained only by explicitly analyzing the specific choice of technique problem which its advent would have presented to objectively dissimilar members of the relevant (historical) population of potential adopters." Come off it.

A lot of economic jargon hides a five-cent thought in a five-dollar word. Economists have forgotten that it's jargon. "Current period responses" means "what people do now"; complex lagged effects" means "the many things they do later." "Interim variation" means "change"; "monitored back" means "told". Economists would think more clearly if they recognized a simple thought for what it is. The "time inconsistency problem" is the economics of changing one's mind. The "principal/agent problem" is the economics of what hirelings do.

The great jargon-generating function in economics is what may be called the Teutonism, such as der Grossjargongeneratingfunktion. German actually invents words like these, with native roots that no doubt make them evocative to German speakers (classical Sanskrit did it, too, using as many as twenty elements). It does not suit the genius of modern

English. "Private wealth-seeking activity" is a knot in the prose. Untie it: "the activity of seeking wealth privately." When laid out in this way, with the liberal use of "of," the phrase looks pretty flabby. "Private" is understood anyway, "Activity of" is pointless (note that nothing happens when you strike it out and reform the phrase). By the principle of untying the knot "the seeking of wealth" is what is left. The unknotting reintroduces "of": "factor price equalization" is muddy, although a strikingly successful bit of mud; "the equalization *of* the prices *of* factors *of* production" is clearer, if straggling. Most teutonisms do not make it as attempts to coin new jargon. "Elastic credit supply expectations rise" is too much to ask of any reader: he must sort out which word goes with which, whether the supply or the expectations are elastic, and what is rising. Hyphens help, but impose more notation. The reader can digest "The long-run balance of payments adjustment" much easier if it's put as "the adjustment of the balance of payments in the long run." The result is inelegant, but no less elegant than the original, and clearer. The following are knots that the reader must untie:

"antiquantity theory evidence"
"contractually uniform transaction cost"
"initial relative capital goods price shock"
"any crude mass expulsion of labor by parliamentary enclosure thesis"
"community decision-making process"
"Cobb-Douglas production function estimation approach"
"alternative property rights schemes"

The possessive, unless attached to a proper noun (Samuelson's genius, Gary's pride), is not used much by good writers. It is overused by poor writers, who delight in phrases like "the standard economist's model." The possessive is a teutonism generator and has the teutonic ambiguity: what is standard, the model or the economist? Sure, you can figure it out: but a writer is not supposed to make puzzles for the reader.

You should re-examine any phrase with more than one adjective, considering whether it might improve if slimmed. Watch especially for nouns used as adjectives. It *is* the genius of English to let verbs become nouns and nouns adjectives.

You go to the club, get a go in cribbage, and hear that all systems are go at the Cape. What is objectionable is piling up these Nounverbadjectives teutonically.

29. *Avoid Cheap Typographical Tricks*

Another objectionable practice is the acronym, such as "Modigliani and Miller (henceforth M&M)" or "purchasing power parity (PPP)." Besides introducing zany associations with candy and second-grade humor, the practice pimples the page and adds a burden of excess notation on the reader. The demands of the computer have worsened the situation. Resist, and remember that even expert mathematicians do not think in symbols. An occasional GNP or CAB won't hurt anyone, but even such a commonplace as GDCF pains all but the most hardened accountant. "Gross domestic capital formation" is fine once or twice to fix ideas, but then "capital formation" or (after all) plain "it" will do the job. Believe me: people will not keep slipping into thinking of it as NDCF or GCF or GC. The point is to be clear, not to "save space" (as the absurd justification for acronyms has it, absurd because the acronyms in most long papers save a half dozen lines of print, less than the table-of-contents paragraph). As usual, good writers set the standard. You won't find them baffling their readers with LQWAGE and BBLUUBB.

Certain other typographical devices need careful handling. Use these "devices" sparingly, they add an "air" of (henceforth "AAO") Breathlessness or Solemnity or *Coyness*! The *point* is that they *add* something, *instead of* "letting it speak for *itself*" (LISFI). They are, so to speak, *sound effects*! The *reader* "understands" this, and doubts *everything* that is said!! LISFI is better. Using these "devices" instead of LISFI suggests that something is wrong with the prose as is. If you use *italics* (underlining) to make your point clear it is probably because the *sentence* is badly set up to give emphasis *naturally*. Fix it. If you use "quotation marks" all the time when not actually "quoting" someone, it is probable that you wish to "apologize" for the "wrong" word or to sneer at "it." Don't. It's impolite to cringe and sneer.

30. *Avoid This, That, These, Those*

Another plague is this-ism. These bad writers think this reader needs repeated reminders that it is *this* idea, not *that* one, which is being discussed. Circle the "this" and "these" in your draft: you'll be surprised at their number. The "this" points the reader back to the thing referred to, for no good reason. No writer wants his reader to look back, for looking back is looking away, interrupting the forward flow and leaving the reader looking for his place. The this-es and thats are demonstrative pronouns on the way to becoming the definite article ("le" and "la" in French come from Latin "ille" and "illa" = "that"; Homeric to Attic Greek went through a similar development). But we already have a definite article. It's called "the." Often plain "the" will do fine, and keep the reader reading. Consider also repeating the word represented by "this." Repetition, remember, brings clarity and unity to English. The rule, then, is to query every "this" or "these." Take most of them out.

31. *Above All, Look at Your Words*

Beyond such matters of taste lies idiom. You must write English, no easy matter. The prepositions of English are its substitute for the grammatical cases that inflected languages have. Prepositions cause trouble. Try experimenting to get them right: is it "by" an increase "of" supply or "because" of an increase "in" supply? God, and Mark Twain, know. Verbs often come preposition-enriched: write down, write up, and the like. Pare the prepositions away if they are not essential. Words often come in couplets: one "overcomes," not "cures," one's ignorance. Thinking in word pairs, on the other hand, leads to the cliché. Flee the cliché when a more original word is more precise and vivid. Observe what varied thoughts about "the pursuit of profit" are suggested by fleeing the cliché: seeking or finding or having or uncovering or coming upon or bumping into profit; and pursuing gain or maximum wealth or opportunities or stimuli or satisfaction or success. New words imply new thoughts. Wordthought is a part of thinking.

One should think what a word literally means and what it connotes. English is jammed with dead metaphors, easily brought to life with incongruous effect. Good writers examine their words for literal meaning, to make sure that the metaphors remain dead or are at the least brought to life in a decorous way. Look at what you have written: are the words literally possible? "The indicators influenced the controls." How does an indicator influence a control? Someone wrote "the severity of the models." Models cannot be "severe." What he meant is that the models make assumptions that are hard to believe. He should have found words to say it.

There is no end to wordlore. Study of dictionaries and style books and the best writing of the age will make you at least embarrassed to be ignorant, the beginning of wisdom. You should probably already know, out of high school, that "however" works better in a secondary position. You should already know that "in this period" is usually redundant, that "not only . . . but also" is a callow Latinism, that "due to" is bureaucratese, that the colon (:) means "to be specific" and the semicolon (;) means "furthermore," that use of "regarding X" or "in regard to X" is definite evidence of a bad education in the language.

Be of good cheer. You have plenty of company in such errors. We all have a lot to learn.

* * * * * *

Good style is above all a matter of taste. Professional economists share with college sophomores the conviction that matters of taste are "mere matters of opinion," the notion being that "opinion" is unarguable. A matter of taste, however, can be argued, often to a conclusion. The best argument is social practice, since that is what taste is. Many people with a claim to know have listed the same rules for writing English, which fact is itself a powerful argument. Mark Twain listed seven rules, familiar now, which would revolutionize economics. The writer must:

1. *Say* what he is proposing to say, not merely come near it.
2. Use the right word, not its second cousin.

3. Eschew surplusage.
4. Not omit necessary details.
5. Avoid slovenliness of form.
6. Use good grammar.
7. Employ a simple and straightforward style.

George Orwell, fifty years later, had got it down to six:

1. Never use a metaphor, simile or other figure of speech which you are used to seeing in print.
2. Never use a long word where a short one will do.
3. If it is possible to cut a word out, always cut it out.
4. Never use the passive where you can use the active.
5. Never use a foreign phrase, a scientific word, or a jargon word if you can think of an everyday English equivalent.
6. Break any of these rules sooner than say anything outright barbarous.

To improve in writing style at all you must become your own harshest editor and grader, as you must become your harshest coach to improve in running or your harshest critic to improve in thinking generally. Good writing is difficult. Economics, however, is too fine a subject to be left in a verbal mess out of mere sloth. What is at first difficult becomes a pleasure in the end, like any skill of civilization.

We can do better, much better, than the say-what-you're-going-to-say, elegant variation, inefficient exposition, boilerplate, incoherent paragraphs, impenetrable tables, unemphatic word order, straggling sentences, contrived triplets, verbosity, nominalization, passive verbs, barbaric neologisms, abstractions, five-dollar words, teutonisms, acronyms, this-es, and fractured idioms of modern economic prose.

Works Cited

BAKER, SHERIDAN and DAVID HAMILTON. 1987. *The Complete Stylist*. New York: Harper & Row.

BARTLETT, JOHN. 1955. *Familiar Quotations*, 13th ed. Boston: Little, Brown.

BARZUN, JACQUES and HENRY F. GRAFF. 1970. *The Modern Researcher*. NY: Harcourt, Brace.

BARZUN, JACQUES. 1976. *Simple and Direct: A Rhetoric for Writers*. NY: Harper & Row.

BECKER, HOWARD S. 1986. *Writing for Social Scientists: How to Start and Finish Your Thesis, Book, or Article*. Chicago: University of Chicago Press.

BOOTH, WAYNE C. 1974. *Modern Dogma and the Rhetoric of Assent*. Chicago: University of Chicago Press.

BOWERSOCK, GLEN W. 1983/1984. "The Art of the Footnote." *The American Scholar* 53: 54–63.

COHEN, J. M. and M. J. COHEN. *The Penguin Dictionary of Modern Quotations*, 2nd ed. Harmondsworth, Middlesex: Penguin.

FOWLER, H. W. 1926 (1965). *Modern English Usage*. Oxford: Oxford University Press.

GALBRAITH, J. K. 1978. "Writing, Typing and Economics." *Atlantic 241* (March): 102–105.

GARDNER, JOHN. 1983. *The Art of Fiction: Notes on Craft for Young Writers*. NY: Knopf.

GOWERS, SIR ERNEST. 1962. *The Complete Plain Words*. London: Penguin.

GRAVES, ROBERT and ALAN HODGE. 1943 (1961). *The Reader Over Your Shoulder: A Handbook for Writers of English Prose*. NY: Macmillan.

HALMOS, PAUL R. 1973. Pp. 19–48 in STEENROD, NORMAN E.

and others, *How to Write Mathematics*. No city: American Mathematics Society.

HALL, DONALD. 1979. *Writing Well*, 3rd ed. Boston: Little, Brown.

JAMES, SIMON. 1984. *A Dictionary of Economic Quotations*. Totowa, NJ: Barnes and Noble.

JORGENSON, DALE. 1966. "The Embodiment Hypothesis." *Journal of Political Economy* 74 (February): 1–17.

LANHAM, RICHARD A. 1987. *Revising Prose*, 2nd ed. NY: Macmillan.

LEWIS, NORMAN. *A Dictionary of Correct Spelling: A Handy Reference Guide*. NY: Barnes and Noble, 1983.

LUCAS, F. L. 1955 (1974). *Style*. London: Cassell.

MACHLUP, FRITZ. 1963 (1967). *Essays in Economic Semantics*. NY: Norton.

McCLOSKEY, D. N. 1985a. *The Rhetoric of Economics*. Madison: University of Wisconsin Press.

———. 1985b. "Economical Writing." *Economic Inquiry* 24 (April): 187–222.

MEDAWAR, PETER. "Is the Scientific Paper Fraudulent?" *Saturday Review* 47 (August 1): 42–43.

MILLS, C. WRIGHT. 1959. "On Intellectual Craftsmanship." In his *The Sociological Imagination*. New York: Grove.

MORGENSTERN, OSKAR. 1963. *On the Accuracy of Economic Observations*, 2nd ed. Princeton: Princeton University Press.

The Oxford Dictionary of Quotations, 2nd ed. 1953. London: Oxford University Press.

OAKESHOTT, MICHAEL. 1933. "Poetry as a Voice in the Conversation of Mankind," in his *Experience and Its Modes*. Reprinted in *Rationalism in Politics*. NY: Basic Books, 1962.

ORWELL, GEORGE. 1946. "Politics and the English Language." Reprinted in Sonia Orwell and Ian Angus, eds. *The Collected Essays, Journalism and Letters of George Orwell*, Vol. IV, *In Front of Your Nose, 1945–1950*. New York: Harcourt Brace Jovanovich, 1968.

PIAGET, JEAN and JEAN-CLAUDE BRINGUIER. 1980. *Conversations with Jean Piaget*. Chicago: University of Chicago Press.

POPPER, KARL. 1976. *Unended Quest: An Intellectual Autobiography*. Glasgow: Collins.

QUINTILIAN. *Institutio Oratoria*. 1980. Cambridge: Harvard University Press.

SALANT, WALTER. 1969. "Writing and Reading in Economics." *Journal of Political Economy* 77 (July/August): 545–558.

SOLOW, ROBERT. 1984. Letter of February 27.

STRUNK, WILLIAM, Jr. and E. B. WHITE. 1959 and later editions. *The Elements of Style*. New York: Macmillan.

TUFTE, EDWARD R. 1983. *The Visual Display of Quantitative Information*. Cheshire, Conn.: Graphics Press.

TWAIN, MARK. 1895. "Fenimore Cooper's Literary Offenses." *The North American Review* (July). Reprinted in *The Unabridged Mark Twain*. Philadelphia: Running Press, 1976.

ULAM, STANISLAW. 1976. *Adventures of a Mathematician*. NY: Scribner's.

Webster's New International Dictionary of the English Language, 2nd ed. 1934. Springfield, Mass.: Merriam.

Webster's New Dictionary of Synonyms. 1973. Springfield, Mass.: Merriam.

Webster's New World Dictionary of the American Language, 2nd college ed. 1976. Cleveland: William Collins & World.

WILLIAMSON, SAMUEL T. 1947. "How to Write Like a Social Scientist." *Saturday Review* 20 (October): 17ff.

WILLIAMS, JOSEPH M. 1981. *Style: Ten Lessons in Clarity and Grace*. Glenview, Ill.: Scott, Foresman.

Index

Index